Thomas Jefferson

Man of the People

By Sonia W. Black

Children's Press®

An Imprint of Scholastic Inc.

Content Consultant
Annette Gordon-Reed, author of the Pulitzer Prize-winning *Hemings of Monticello: An American Family* and
Professor of History, Faculty of Arts and Sciences, Harvard University

Thank you to Jevon Bolden for her insights into African American history and culture.

Library of Congress Catalog-in-Publication Data
Names: Black, Sonia W., author.
Title: Thomas Jefferson: man of the people/Sonia W. Black.
Description: New York: Children's Press, an imprint of Scholastic, Inc., [2021] | Series: Presidential biographies | Includes index. | Audience: Ages 7–9. | Audience: Grades 2–3. | Summary: "Book introduces the reader to Thomas Jefferson and his life." —Provided by publisher.
Identifiers: LCCN 2020002645 | ISBN 9780531130964 (library binding) | ISBN 9780531130681 (paperback)
Subjects: LCSH: Jefferson, Thomas, 1743–1826—Juvenile literature. | Lewis and Clark Expedition (1804–1806)—Juvenile literature. | Presidents—United States—Biography—Juvenile literature. | United States—History—1783–1815—Juvenile literature.
Classification: LCC E332.79 .B55 2021 | DDC 973.4/6092 [B]—dc23
LC record available at https://lccn.loc.gov/2020002645

Initial prototype design by Anna Tunick Tabachnik
Produced by Spooky Cheetah Press
Design by Kimberly Shake

Printed in North Mankato, MN, USA 113

SCHOLASTIC, CHILDREN'S PRESS, PRESIDENTIAL BIOGRAPHIES™, and associated logos
are trademarks and/or registered trademarks of Scholastic Inc.

1 2 3 4 5 6 7 8 9 10 R 30 29 28 27 26 25 24 23 22 21

Scholastic Inc., 557 Broadway, New York, NY 10012.

Photos ©: cover, spine: GraphicaArtis/Getty Images; back cover: World History Archive/Superstock; 4 and throughout: Universal History Archive/UIG/Shutterstock; 5: Superstock, Inc.; 6: Pamela Patrick White/White Historic Art; 8: Silverfish Press/National Geographic Image Collection/Bridgeman Images; 10: World History Archive/Superstock; 11: The Granger Collection; 13: Look and Learn/Bridgeman Images; 14: Nawrocki/ClassicStock/Getty Images; 16: Look and Learn/Bridgeman Images; 18: Sarin Images/The Granger Collection; 22: Jim McMahon/Mapman®; 26: Mark Summerfield/Alamy Images; 28: The Granger Collection; 29 all: North Wind Picture Archives/Alamy Images; 30 top left: Superstock, Inc.; 30 top right: Look and Learn/Bridgeman Images; 30 bottom: World History Archive/Superstock; 31 top left: The Granger Collection; 31 bottom left: Sarin Images/The Granger Collection. All other photos © Shutterstock.

SOURCE NOTES: Page 5: "From Thomas Jefferson to Peter Carr, 19 August 1785," Founders Online, National Archives, https://founders.archives.gov/documents/Jefferson/01-08-02-0319; page 6: Thomas Jefferson to John Adams, June 10, 1815, manuscript/mixed material, retrieved from the Library of Congress, https://www.loc.gov/item/mtjbib022062/; page 10: Thomas Jefferson, Rough Draft of the Declaration of Independence, June 1776, manuscript/mixed material, retrieved from the Library of Congress, https://www.loc.gov/item/mtjbib000156/; page 16: "From Thomas Jefferson to John Adams, 25 April 1794," Founders Online, National Archives, accessed September 29, 2019, https://founders.archives.gov/documents/Jefferson/01-28-02-0055; page 21: "From Thomas Jefferson to Martha Jefferson, 5 May 1787," Founders Online, National Archives, accessed September 29, 2019, https://founders.archives.gov/documents/Jefferson/01-11-02-0327.

COVER: A portrait of President Jefferson.

Table of Contents

CHAPTER 1

Meet Thomas Jefferson

Thomas Jefferson had many talents. He was a lawyer and a musician. He designed buildings and was an excellent writer. In fact, Jefferson wrote the Declaration of Independence. That document helped free the 13 American **colonies** from British rule. Jefferson was also the third president of the United States. During his first **term**, he nearly doubled the size of the country.

Jefferson came from a wealthy family. He owned a lot of property and held many **enslaved** people. He collected many books and works of art. Yet Jefferson spent his career making sure the government represented the common man. He had very big dreams for his country and worked hard to see them through.

Jefferson was 57 years old when he was elected president.

"[W]henever you are to do a thing . . . ask yourself how you would act were all the world looking at you, & act accordingly."

—Thomas Jefferson, August 19, 1785

Jefferson's love of books—and of learning—continued throughout his life.

"I cannot live without books."
—Thomas Jefferson, June 10, 1815

Jefferson's Early Years

Shy, quiet Thomas Jefferson was born on April 13, 1743. He was one of ten children. The Jeffersons lived in Virginia—the largest of the 13 British colonies in America. Thomas grew up on a large **plantation**.

The Jeffersons' house was filled with books and musical instruments. As a youngster, Thomas enjoyed reading, writing compositions, and playing the violin. He also loved to go exploring outside.

At first, Thomas was taught in a little schoolhouse on the plantation with his siblings. At age nine, he was sent to boarding school. There, Thomas studied French, Latin, and Greek. He was always excited to learn new things.

Young Jefferson often practiced violin for three hours a day.

Jefferson designed Monticello. Enslaved people, who had no rights and worked without pay, built it.

Monticello means "little mountain" in Italian.

8

Building a New Life

When Jefferson was just 14 years old, his father died. Jefferson was given his father's books, desk, and bookcases. He also took possession of the family plantation and its many enslaved African Americans.

When he was 16 years old, Jefferson began attending college in Williamsburg, Virginia. Later, he studied to be a lawyer. Jefferson was a hard worker. By 1767, he had his own law practice.

In 1768, Jefferson decided to build his own house on the family land, high on a hill. He drew designs for the house, and his laborers began building. Jefferson named his house Monticello.

On New Year's Day in 1772, 29-year-old Thomas married 23-year-old Martha Wayles Skelton. They started their new life at Monticello.

Benjamin Franklin (left) and John Adams (center) worked on the Declaration with Jefferson (right).

"We hold these truths to be self-evident, that all men are created equal. . . ."
—Declaration of Independence, 1776

Writing the Declaration

It was a tense time in America. Colonists were unhappy with British rule. Eventually, they decided to fight for their freedom. The first shots of the American Revolution were fired in April 1775. One year later, colonial leaders decided to draft the Declaration of Independence. Because Jefferson was an excellent writer, they choose him to write the document. Then it was presented to the king of England, George III.

In the Declaration, Jefferson explained why the colonies should be free. He also outlined rights he envisioned for Americans. These rights applied to white men with property. The poor, women, and people of color were most often left out.

Jefferson designed this desk, which he used while writing the Declaration.

CHAPTER 2

A Growing Leader

Jefferson also wrote new laws to help the colonists. He kept working toward America's freedom. In 1779, he was elected governor of Virginia.

The Declaration of Independence had been delivered to the king of England. But that didn't bring freedom to the colonies. It didn't end the war. General George Washington led the Continental Army. The colonists battled British forces for a total of eight bloody years. Finally, with help from France, American troops defeated the British forces at Yorktown, Virginia, in October 1781. Battles would continue to be fought at sea for two more years. But the outcome had become clear. America would soon be free.

On October 19, 1781, British general Cornwallis (left) surrendered to General George Washington (right).

Jefferson wrote many things. But he wrote only one book. *Notes on the State of Virginia* was published in 1787.

Like her husband, Martha Jefferson was said to be a talented musician.

14

Family Life at Monticello

Jefferson's second term as governor ended in 1781. He didn't want to run again. Instead, Jefferson retired to spend time at home with his family.

Over the years, Jefferson had continued to grow his estate. He fought hard for the freedom of the American colonists. Yet over his lifetime, Jefferson held about 600 enslaved people who were treated as property. Jefferson may have struggled with the idea of slavery. But he didn't think he could run his large plantation without the labor of enslaved workers.

Jefferson's time at home with his family was cut short in 1782. His wife died after giving birth to their sixth child. One year later, the American Revolution officially ended. American leaders asked Jefferson to represent the nation in France. He moved to Paris in 1784.

About 1,000 people participated in the storming of the Bastille.

"I have seen enough of one war never to wish to see another."
—Thomas Jefferson, April 25, 1794

A Return to Politics

Jefferson was a minister to France. The new United States government had to form relationships with other countries. Jefferson lived in France for five years. He worked on trade agreements with other countries. During that time, Jefferson grew to love French culture.

He also saw the French people become more unhappy with their rulers. King Louis XVI taxed the French citizens heavily. The people were getting poorer. But the king and his wife lived a rich life. On July 14, 1789, angry citizens attacked a government fort called the Bastille. They took gunpowder for their weapons. The French Revolution had begun. Citizens fought for fair and equal treatment from the government. For Jefferson, it was a reminder of what Americans had fought for.

After leaving his boardinghouse, Jefferson (right) walked to his inauguration.

Jefferson was a shy public speaker. He spoke so softly, many people in the room were unable to hear his inauguration speech.

The Path to the Presidency

Jefferson returned to the United States in 1789. George Washington was president. He asked Jefferson to serve as secretary of state. Jefferson accepted and, for the next five years, he continued to work on building America's relationships with other nations.

Washington decided to retire when his second term ended in 1797. That year, Jefferson ran for president. But he lost to John Adams, who became our country's second president. Jefferson was Adams's vice president. Jefferson ran again in 1800. This time he won. He became the third president of the United States. He was **inaugurated** on March 4, 1801.

The American flag had 15 stars when Jefferson was president. ▶

CHAPTER 3

Life in the White House

On March 19, 1801, President Jefferson moved into the White House. He did not like large, formal parties. Instead, Jefferson enjoyed inviting small groups of guests for comfortable get-togethers. He'd often play the violin to entertain them.

Jefferson's curious nature had continued into adulthood. He was fascinated with an **extinct** animal called the great mammoth. He collected **fossils** of its teeth. Scientists once found the bones of a great mammoth and sent them to Jefferson. The president spent hours piecing the bones together.

This is an illustration of a great mammoth skeleton. ▶

Jefferson helped make ice cream popular in the United States. He often had it served to visitors at the White House.

"It is wonderful how much may be done, if we are always doing."
—Thomas Jefferson, May 5, 1787

The Louisiana Purchase, 1803

This map shows North America in 1803 and the land that was added through the Louisiana Purchase.

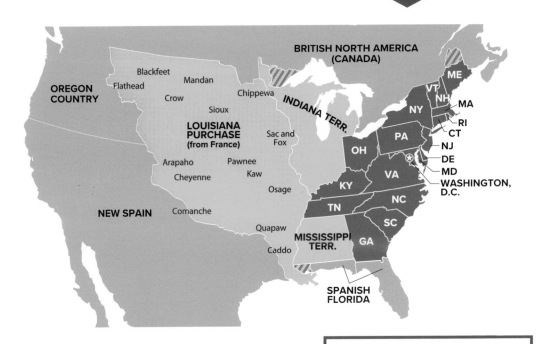

BRITISH NORTH AMERICA (CANADA)

OREGON COUNTRY

Blackfeet
Flathead
Mandan
Crow
Sioux
Chippewa

INDIANA TERR.

LOUISIANA PURCHASE (from France)

Sac and Fox

Arapaho
Cheyenne
Pawnee
Kaw
Osage

NEW SPAIN

Comanche

Quapaw
Caddo

MISSISSIPPI TERR.

SPANISH FLORIDA

ME
VT
NH
NY
MA
RI
CT
PA
NJ
OH
DE
MD
VA
WASHINGTON, D.C.
KY
TN
NC
SC
GA

The new lands stretched from the Mississippi River to the Rocky Mountains.

KEY

■ U.S. state
■ U.S. territory
▨ Disputed area
● Other territories
Sioux Some of the main Native Nations living in the Purchase area

The Louisiana Purchase

In 1803, President Jefferson bought the Louisiana Territory from France. He paid 15 million dollars.

The Louisiana Purchase had many benefits for Americans. It nearly doubled the size of the United States. The population of the country had been growing. Most people lived along the coast. Now they could start moving west. The Mississippi River was located in the new territory. Now Americans could travel freely on the river.

The Louisiana Purchase caused a lot of harm, too—specifically to Indigenous Peoples. Many nations lived in the area. They'd been there for thousands of years. Struggles arose between the Indigenous people and the new settlers. Over the years, white settlers continued to push the Indigenous people off their land.

Monticello is now a museum. More than 500,000 people visit it every year.

It took about 40 years to complete Monticello. The house grew from 14 to 33 rooms and there were another 10 rooms around it.

The End of an Era

In 1804, Jefferson won a second term. France and England were at war. France had helped America in its war for independence. But Jefferson did not take sides in this war. Napoleon, the French leader, got angry. He stopped all shipping trade with America. Then Jefferson passed the Embargo Act. That stopped U.S. trade with France and other nations. That hurt American businesses. People were angry. In 1809, Jefferson signed a new act that again allowed most overseas trade. His term as president ended that year.

Jefferson retired to Monticello. The grand estate now included a factory, stables, flower gardens, vegetable gardens, and orchards. It was also home to the four children Jefferson had with Sally Hemings, an enslaved woman at Monticello.

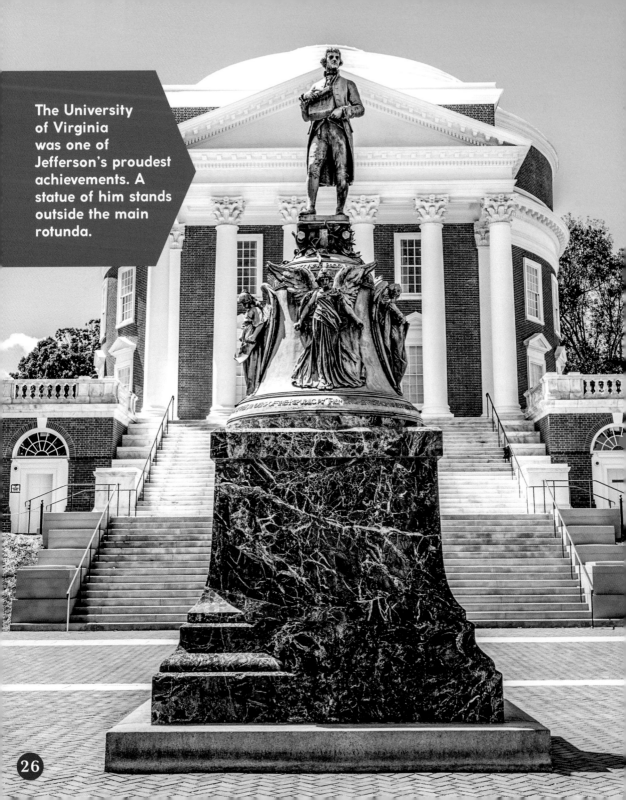

The University of Virginia was one of Jefferson's proudest achievements. A statue of him stands outside the main rotunda.

Expanding Education

Now Jefferson set his sights on a new goal: free public education. This was a completely new idea for the time. Rich young white boys and men filled most schools at the time. Jefferson wanted to make public school available to boys and men of all social classes. This did not include women or people of color.

Jefferson worked on founding a state university in Virginia. He even drew the plans for the building. Construction began in 1817. Eight years later, on March 7, 1825, the University of Virginia opened.

Jefferson died one year later, on July 4, 1826. It was the 50th anniversary of the Declaration of Independence.

President Jefferson (second from left) is represented on Mount Rushmore.

The Lewis and Clark Expedition

Thomas Jefferson wanted to learn all about the nation's land in the Louisiana Territory. In 1804, he sent Meriwether Lewis and William Clark to explore the area and the Pacific Northwest. Their team included carpenters, boatmen, and blacksmiths. Along the way, they met an Indigenous woman of the Shoshone nation. Her name was Sacagawea (sa-kuh-guh-WEE-uh). Sacagawea became

Sacagawea had a baby that she carried on her back for most of the trip.

The explorers detailed what they saw and who they met in their journals.

their guide. She helped Lewis and Clark talk to and make friends with the various Indigenous people they met. She also taught them how to find and prepare food. It is doubtful the expedition would have succeeded without her help. The exploration ended in 1806. By then, the explorers had identified almost 200 plants and more than 100 animals that white people had never seen before. They blazed a trail from the Mississippi River to the Pacific Ocean. In the years that followed, many Americans moved to settle in the West.

American History

1744
King George's War, a struggle between Great Britain and France over territory in North America, begins in May. It lasts until 1748.

1773
On December 16, colonists dump tea into Boston Harbor to protest taxes. The Boston Tea Party results in more laws that increase tensions between England and the colonies.

1775
On April 19, the first battle of the American Revolution takes place at Lexington and Concord in Massachusetts. The war ends eight years later, on September 3, 1783, with the Treaty of Paris. The United States officially becomes a country.

1743 > **1744** > **1772** > **1773** > **1775** > **1776**

1743
On April 13, Thomas Jefferson is born in the colony of Virginia.

1772
Jefferson marries Martha Wayles Skelton on January 1. They will have six children together.

1776
Jefferson spends 17 days writing the Declaration of Independence and two days revising it before it is approved on July 4.

Thomas Jefferson's Life

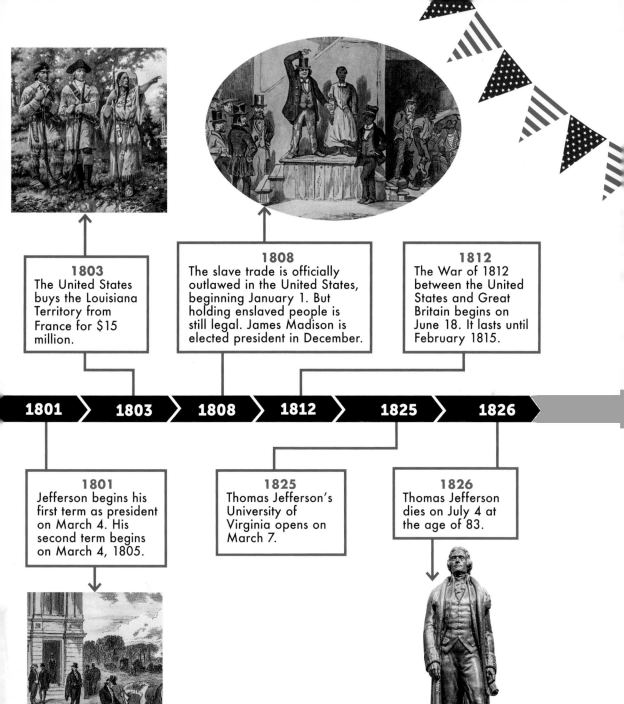

1803
The United States buys the Louisiana Territory from France for $15 million.

1808
The slave trade is officially outlawed in the United States, beginning January 1. But holding enslaved people is still legal. James Madison is elected president in December.

1812
The War of 1812 between the United States and Great Britain begins on June 18. It lasts until February 1815.

1801 〉 **1803** 〉 **1808** 〉 **1812** 〉 **1825** 〉 **1826**

1801
Jefferson begins his first term as president on March 4. His second term begins on March 4, 1805.

1825
Thomas Jefferson's University of Virginia opens on March 7.

1826
Thomas Jefferson dies on July 4 at the age of 83.

GLOSSARY

colonies (KAH-luh-neez): territories that have been settled by people from another country and are controlled by that country

enslaved (en-SLAYVD): held by another person and thought of as property, without the right of fair treatment

extinct (ik-STINGKIT): no longer found alive

fossils (FOSS-uhls): the remains or traces of an animal or plant from millions of years ago, preserved as rock

inaugurated (in-aw-gyuh-RAY-ted): sworn into office

plantation (plan-TAY-shuhun): a large farm found in warm climates where crops such as tobacco, rubber trees, and cotton are grown

term (TURM): a definite or limited period of time

INDEX

ABOUT THE AUTHOR

Sonia W. Black is a former editor at Scholastic. She has worked on books in a range of formats, from picture books to young adult novels. Ms. Black is also the author of a number of titles for early readers. She lives in New Jersey.